Gratitude Journal

First published in 2018 by Erin Rose Publishing

Text and illustration copyright © 2019 Erin Rose Publishing

Design: Julie Anson

Behind every successful woman
is a tribe of other successful
women who have her back.

Gratitude Journal

Date: ....

❋ Today I am grateful for:

....
....
....
....
....

☀ What are my challenges?

....
....
....
....
....

☆ What would I like to achieve?

....
....
....
....
....

◠ Positive daily affirmation: I am...

....
....
....
....
....

Gratitude Journal

Date: ....

✳ Today I am grateful for:

....

....

....

....

....

☀ What are my challenges?

....

....

....

....

☆ What would I like to achieve?

....

....

....

....

🌈 Positive daily affirmation: I am...

....

....

....

....

....

Gratitude Journal

Date: ....

❀ Today I am grateful for:

....
....
....
....
....

☀ What are my challenges?

....
....
....
....

☆ What would I like to achieve?

....
....
....
....

🌈 Positive daily affirmation: I am...

....
....
....
....

Gratitude Journal

Date: ....

✳ Today I am grateful for:

....
....
....
....
....

☀ What are my challenges?

....
....
....
....
....

☆ What would I like to achieve?

....
....
....
....
....

🌈 Positive daily affirmation: I am...

....
....
....
....
....

Gratitude Journal

Date: ....

❀ Today I am grateful for:

....
....
....
....
....
....

☀ What are my challenges?

....
....
....
....
....

☆ What would I like to achieve?

....
....
....
....
....

🌈 Positive daily affirmation: I am...

....
....
....
....
....
....

Gratitude Journal

Date: ....

❋ Today I am grateful for:

....
....
....
....
....

☀ What are my challenges?

....
....
....
....
....

☆ What would I like to achieve?

....
....
....
....
....

🌈 Positive daily affirmation: I am...

....
....
....
....
....
....

Gratitude Journal

Date: ....

❋ Today I am grateful for:

....

....

....

....

....

☀ What are my challenges?

....

....

....

....

☆ What would I like to achieve?

....

....

....

....

🌈 Positive daily affirmation: I am...

....

....

....

....

....

Gratitude Journal

Date: ....

❋ Today I am grateful for:

....

....

....

....

....

....

☀ What are my challenges?

....

....

....

....

....

☆ What would I like to achieve?

....

....

....

....

....

◠ Positive daily affirmation: I am...

....

....

....

....

....

....

....

Gratitude Journal

Date: ....

❀ Today I am grateful for:

....
....
....
....
....

☀ What are my challenges?

....
....
....
....
....

☆ What would I like to achieve?

....
....
....
....
....

🌈 Positive daily affirmation: I am...

....
....
....
....
....

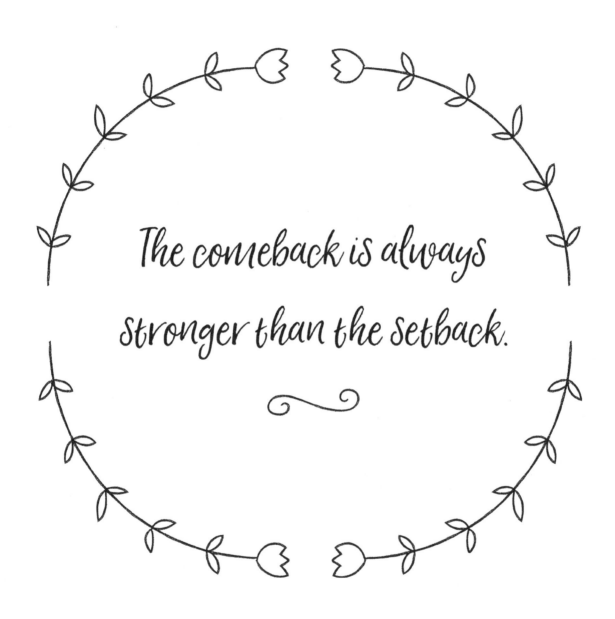

The comeback is always stronger than the setback.

Gratitude Journal

Date: ....

❋ Today I am grateful for:

....
....
....
....
....
....

☀ What are my challenges?

....
....
....
....
....
....

☆ What would I like to achieve?

....
....
....
....
....

🌈 Positive daily affirmation: I am...

....
....
....
....
....

Gratitude Journal

Date: ....

❇ Today I am grateful for:

....
....
....
....
....
....

☼ What are my challenges?

....
....
....
....
....

☆ What would I like to achieve?

....
....
....
....
....

🌈 Positive daily affirmation: I am...

....
....
....
....
....

Gratitude Journal

Date: ....

✽ Today I am grateful for:

....
....
....
....
....
....

☀ What are my challenges?

....
....
....
....
....
....

☆ What would I like to achieve?

....
....
....
....
....
....

⌒ Positive daily affirmation: I am...

....
....
....
....
....
....

Gratitude Journal

Date: ....

❀ Today I am grateful for:

....
....
....
....
....
....

☀ What are my challenges?

....
....
....
....
....

☆ What would I like to achieve?

....
....
....
....
....

🌈 Positive daily affirmation: I am...

....
....
....
....
....

Gratitude Journal

Date: ....

✳ Today I am grateful for:

....
....
....
....
....

☀ What are my challenges?

....
....
....
....
....

☆ What would I like to achieve?

....
....
....
....
....

🌈 Positive daily affirmation: I am...

....
....
....
....
....

A woman is unstoppable after she realises she deserves better.

Gratitude Journal

Date: ....

❋ Today I am grateful for:

....
....
....
....
....

☀ What are my challenges?

....
....
....
....
....

☆ What would I like to achieve?

....
....
....
....
....

🌈 Positive daily affirmation: I am...

....
....
....
....
....

Gratitude Journal

Date: ....

❋ Today I am grateful for:

....
....
....
....
....

☀ What are my challenges?

....
....
....
....
....

☆ What would I like to achieve?

....
....
....
....
....

◠ Positive daily affirmation: I am...

....
....
....
....
....

Gratitude Journal

Date: ....

✳ Today I am grateful for:

....

....

....

....

....

☀ What are my challenges?

....

....

....

....

....

☆ What would I like to achieve?

....

....

....

....

....

🌈 Positive daily affirmation: I am...

....

....

....

....

....

Gratitude Journal

Date: ....

❀ Today I am grateful for:

....
....
....
....
....
....

☀ What are my challenges?

....
....
....
....
....

☆ What would I like to achieve?

....
....
....
....
....

🌈 Positive daily affirmation: I am...

....
....
....
....
....
....

Gratitude Journal

Date: ....

✳ Today I am grateful for:

....

....

....

....

....

....

☀ What are my challenges?

....

....

....

....

....

....

☆ What would I like to achieve?

....

....

....

....

....

....

🌈 Positive daily affirmation: I am...

....

....

....

....

....

....

If you obey all the rules
you miss all the fun

~KATHARINE HEPBURN

Gratitude Journal

Date: ....

✳ Today I am grateful for:

....
....
....
....
....

☀ What are my challenges?

....
....
....
....
....

☆ What would I like to achieve?

....
....
....
....
....

🌈 Positive daily affirmation: I am...

....
....
....
....
....
....

Gratitude Journal

Date: ....

❋ Today I am grateful for:

....
....
....
....
....
....

☀ What are my challenges?

....
....
....
....
....

☆ What would I like to achieve?

....
....
....
....
....

◠ Positive daily affirmation: I am...

....
....
....
....
....
....

Gratitude Journal

Date: ....

❀ Today I am grateful for:

....
....
....
....
....
....

☀ What are my challenges?

....
....
....
....
....
....

☆ What would I like to achieve?

....
....
....
....
....
....

🌈 Positive daily affirmation: I am...

....
....
....
....
....
....

Gratitude Journal

Date: ....

❀ Today I am grateful for:

....

....

....

....

....

....

☀ What are my challenges?

....

....

....

....

....

....

☆ What would I like to achieve?

....

....

....

....

....

....

🌈 Positive daily affirmation: I am...

....

....

....

....

....

....

Gratitude Journal

Date: ....

❋ Today I am grateful for:

....
....
....
....
....
....

☀ What are my challenges?

....
....
....
....
....
....

☆ What would I like to achieve?

....
....
....
....
....
....

◠ Positive daily affirmation: I am...

....
....
....
....
....
....

Be fearless in the pursuit
of what sets your soul on fire.

Gratitude Journal

Date: ....

❋ Today I am grateful for:

....
....
....
....
....

☀ What are my challenges?

....
....
....
....
....

☆ What would I like to achieve?

....
....
....
....
....

🌈 Positive daily affirmation: I am...

....
....
....
....
....

Gratitude Journal

Date: ....

✻ Today I am grateful for:

....
....
....
....
....
....

☀ What are my challenges?

....
....
....
....
....
....

☆ What would I like to achieve?

....
....
....
....
....
....

🌈 Positive daily affirmation: I am...

....
....
....
....
....
....

Gratitude Journal

Date: ....

✿ Today I am grateful for:

....
....
....
....
....

☀ What are my challenges?

....
....
....
....
....

☆ What would I like to achieve?

....
....
....
....
....

🌈 Positive daily affirmation: I am...

....
....
....
....
....

Gratitude Journal

Date: ....

Today I am grateful for:

What are my challenges?

What would I like to achieve?

Positive daily affirmation: I am...

Gratitude Journal

Date: ....

❋ Today I am grateful for:

....

....

....

....

....

....

☀ What are my challenges?

....

....

....

....

....

....

☆ What would I like to achieve?

....

....

....

....

....

....

◠ Positive daily affirmation: I am...

....

....

....

....

....

....

Sometimes you have to fake
it until you make it!

Gratitude Journal

Date: ....

✻ Today I am grateful for:

....
....
....
....
....
....

☀ What are my challenges?

....
....
....
....
....
....

☆ What would I like to achieve?

....
....
....
....
....
....

🌈 Positive daily affirmation: I am...

....
....
....
....
....

Gratitude Journal

Date: ....

❀ Today I am grateful for:

....
....
....
....
....
....

☀ What are my challenges?

....
....
....
....
....
....

☆ What would I like to achieve?

....
....
....
....
....

🌈 Positive daily affirmation: I am...

....
....
....
....
....
....

Gratitude Journal

Date: ....

Today I am grateful for:

What are my challenges?

What would I like to achieve?

Positive daily affirmation: I am...

Gratitude Journal

Date: ....

❀ Today I am grateful for:

....
....
....
....
....

☀ What are my challenges?

....
....
....
....
....

☆ What would I like to achieve?

....
....
....
....
....

◠ Positive daily affirmation: I am...

....
....
....
....
....
....

Gratitude Journal

Date: ....

✻ Today I am grateful for:

....
....
....
....
....
....

☀ What are my challenges?

....
....
....
....
....
....

☆ What would I like to achieve?

....
....
....
....
....
....

🌈 Positive daily affirmation: I am...

....
....
....
....
....

Limitations are the illusions which keep you from being great.

Gratitude Journal

Date: ....

❀ Today I am grateful for:

....
....
....
....
....

☼ What are my challenges?

....
....
....
....
....

☆ What would I like to achieve?

....
....
....
....
....

🌈 Positive daily affirmation: I am...

....
....
....
....
....
....

Gratitude Journal

Date: ....

❊ Today I am grateful for:

....

....

....

....

....

☀ What are my challenges?

....

....

....

....

....

☆ What would I like to achieve?

....

....

....

....

....

◠ Positive daily affirmation: I am...

....

....

....

....

....

Gratitude Journal

Date: ....

✻ Today I am grateful for:

....
....
....
....
....
....

☼ What are my challenges?

....
....
....
....
....

☆ What would I like to achieve?

....
....
....
....
....

🌈 Positive daily affirmation: I am...

....
....
....
....
....
....

Gratitude Journal

Date: ....

✼ Today I am grateful for:

....
....
....
....
....
....

☀ What are my challenges?

....
....
....
....
....

☆ What would I like to achieve?

....
....
....
....
....

🌈 Positive daily affirmation: I am...

....
....
....
....
....

Gratitude Journal

Date: ....

✻ Today I am grateful for:

....
....
....
....
....

☀ What are my challenges?

....
....
....
....
....

☆ What would I like to achieve?

....
....
....
....
....

🌈 Positive daily affirmation: I am...

....
....
....
....
....

Believe in yourself and avoid
anyone who undermines you.

Gratitude Journal

Date: ....

❀ Today I am grateful for:

....

....

....

....

....

....

☀ What are my challenges?

....

....

....

....

....

....

☆ What would I like to achieve?

....

....

....

....

....

◠ Positive daily affirmation: I am...

....

....

....

....

....

....

Gratitude Journal

Date: ....

❈ *Today I am grateful for:*

....

....

....

....

....

☀ *What are my challenges?*

....

....

....

....

....

☆ *What would I like to achieve?*

....

....

....

....

....

🌈 *Positive daily affirmation: I am...*

....

....

....

....

....

Gratitude Journal

Date: ....

✽ Today I am grateful for:

....
....
....
....
....

☀ What are my challenges?

....
....
....
....
....
....

☆ What would I like to achieve?

....
....
....
....
....

🌈 Positive daily affirmation: I am...

....
....
....
....
....
....

Gratitude Journal

Date: ....

❀ Today I am grateful for:
....
....
....
....
....

☀ What are my challenges?
....
....
....
....
....

☆ What would I like to achieve?
....
....
....
....
....

🌈 Positive daily affirmation: I am...
....
....
....
....
....

Gratitude Journal

Date: ....

✽ Today I am grateful for:

....
....
....
....
....

☀ What are my challenges?

....
....
....
....
....

☆ What would I like to achieve?

....
....
....
....
....

🌈 Positive daily affirmation: I am...

....
....
....
....
....

The best way to gain self-confidence is to do what you are afraid to do

~SWATI SHARMA

Gratitude Journal

Date: ....

❋ Today I am grateful for:

....
....
....
....
....

☀ What are my challenges?

....
....
....
....
....

☆ What would I like to achieve?

....
....
....
....
....

🌈 Positive daily affirmation: I am...

....
....
....
....
....

Gratitude Journal

Date: ....

❀ Today I am grateful for:

....
....
....
....
....
....

☀ What are my challenges?

....
....
....
....
....
....

☆ What would I like to achieve?

....
....
....
....
....
....

◠ Positive daily affirmation: I am...

....
....
....
....
....
....

Gratitude Journal

Date: ....

❋ Today I am grateful for:

....
....
....
....
....

☀ What are my challenges?

....
....
....
....
....

☆ What would I like to achieve?

....
....
....
....

🌈 Positive daily affirmation: I am...

....
....
....
....
....

Gratitude Journal

Date: ....

✻ Today I am grateful for:

....
....
....
....
....

☀ What are my challenges?

....
....
....
....
....

☆ What would I like to achieve?

....
....
....
....
....

🌈 Positive daily affirmation: I am...

....
....
....
....
....

Gratitude Journal

Date: ....

Today I am grateful for:

What are my challenges?

What would I like to achieve?

Positive daily affirmation: I am...

Don't worry, just breathe.
If it's meant to be
it will find a way.

Gratitude Journal

Date: ....

❁ Today I am grateful for:

....

....

....

....

....

....

☀ What are my challenges?

....

....

....

....

....

☆ What would I like to achieve?

....

....

....

....

....

⌒ Positive daily affirmation: I am...

....

....

....

....

....

....

Gratitude Journal

Date: ....

✳ Today I am grateful for:

....
....
....
....
....

☀ What are my challenges?

....
....
....
....
....

☆ What would I like to achieve?

....
....
....
....
....

🌈 Positive daily affirmation: I am...

....
....
....
....
....

Gratitude Journal

Date: ....

✹ Today I am grateful for:

....
....
....
....
....

☀ What are my challenges?

....
....
....
....
....

☆ What would I like to achieve?

....
....
....
....
....

🌈 Positive daily affirmation: I am...

....
....
....
....
....

Gratitude Journal

Date: ....

✽ Today I am grateful for:
....
....
....
....
....

☀ What are my challenges?
....
....
....
....
....

☆ What would I like to achieve?
....
....
....
....
....

🌈 Positive daily affirmation: I am...
....
....
....
....
....

Gratitude Journal

Date: ....

✾ Today I am grateful for:

....
....
....
....
....

☀ What are my challenges?

....
....
....
....
....

☆ What would I like to achieve?

....
....
....
....
....

◠ Positive daily affirmation: I am...

....
....
....
....
....

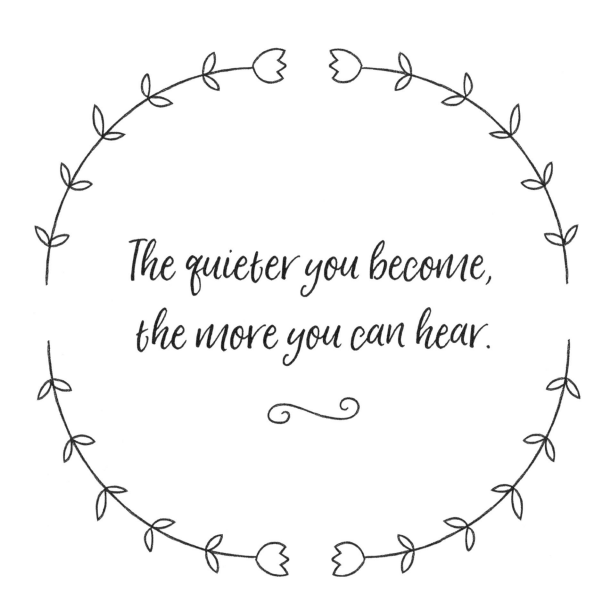

The quieter you become,
the more you can hear.

Gratitude Journal

Date: ....

✽ Today I am grateful for:

....
....
....
....
....

☀ What are my challenges?

....
....
....
....
....

☆ What would I like to achieve?

....
....
....
....
....

🌈 Positive daily affirmation: I am...

....
....
....
....
....

Gratitude Journal

Date: ....

✽ Today I am grateful for:

....

....

....

....

....

....

☀ What are my challenges?

....

....

....

....

....

☆ What would I like to achieve?

....

....

....

....

....

◠ Positive daily affirmation: I am...

....

....

....

....

....

....

Gratitude Journal

Date: ....

❋ Today I am grateful for:

....
....
....
....
....

☀ What are my challenges?

....
....
....
....
....

☆ What would I like to achieve?

....
....
....
....
....

🌈 Positive daily affirmation: I am...

....
....
....
....
....
....

Gratitude Journal

Date: ....

❀ Today I am grateful for:

....
....
....
....
....
....

☀ What are my challenges?

....
....
....
....
....
....

☆ What would I like to achieve?

....
....
....
....
....
....

🌈 Positive daily affirmation: I am...

....
....
....
....
....
....

Gratitude Journal

Date: ....

❋ Today I am grateful for:

....
....
....
....
....

☀ What are my challenges?

....
....
....
....
....

☆ What would I like to achieve?

....
....
....
....
....

🌈 Positive daily affirmation: I am...

....
....
....
....
....

It's okay not to have
all the answers.

Gratitude Journal

Date: ....

✵ Today I am grateful for:

....

....

....

....

....

☀ What are my challenges?

....

....

....

....

....

☆ What would I like to achieve?

....

....

....

....

....

🌈 Positive daily affirmation: I am...

....

....

....

....

....

Gratitude Journal

Date: ....

❁ Today I am grateful for:

....

....

....

....

....

☀ What are my challenges?

....

....

....

....

☆ What would I like to achieve?

....

....

....

....

◠ Positive daily affirmation: I am...

....

....

....

....

....

Gratitude Journal

Date: ....

✻ Today I am grateful for:

....
....
....
....
....
....

☀ What are my challenges?

....
....
....
....
....
....

☆ What would I like to achieve?

....
....
....
....
....
....

🌈 Positive daily affirmation: I am...

....
....
....
....
....
....

Gratitude Journal

Date: ....

❋ Today I am grateful for:

....
....
....
....
....
....

☀ What are my challenges?

....
....
....
....
....

☆ What would I like to achieve?

....
....
....
....
....

🌈 Positive daily affirmation: I am...

....
....
....
....
....
....

Gratitude Journal

Date: ....

❋ Today I am grateful for:

....
....
....
....
....

☀ What are my challenges?

....
....
....
....
....

☆ What would I like to achieve?

....
....
....
....
....

🌈 Positive daily affirmation: I am...

....
....
....
....
....

In the midst of movement
and chaos, keep stillness
inside of you

Gratitude Journal

Date: ....

❋ Today I am grateful for:

....
....
....
....
....

☀ What are my challenges?

....
....
....
....
....

☆ What would I like to achieve?

....
....
....
....
....

🌈 Positive daily affirmation: I am...

....
....
....
....
....

Gratitude Journal

Date: ....

✽ Today I am grateful for:

....
....
....
....
....
....

☀ What are my challenges?

....
....
....
....
....
....

☆ What would I like to achieve?

....
....
....
....
....

〰 Positive daily affirmation: I am...

....
....
....
....
....
....

Gratitude Journal

Date: ....

✤ Today I am grateful for:

....
....
....
....
....

☀ What are my challenges?

....
....
....
....
....

☆ What would I like to achieve?

....
....
....
....
....

🌈 Positive daily affirmation: I am...

....
....
....
....
....
....

Gratitude Journal

Date: ....

✽ Today I am grateful for:

....
....
....
....
....
....

☀ What are my challenges?

....
....
....
....
....
....

☆ What would I like to achieve?

....
....
....
....
....
....

🌈 Positive daily affirmation: I am...

....
....
....
....
....
....

Gratitude Journal

Date: ....

❈ Today I am grateful for:

....
....
....
....
....
....

☀ What are my challenges?

....
....
....
....
....
....

☆ What would I like to achieve?

....
....
....
....
....
....

◠ Positive daily affirmation: I am...

....
....
....
....
....

There are far better things ahead than any we leave behind.

~C.S LEWIS

Gratitude Journal

Date: ....

✳ Today I am grateful for:

....
....
....
....
....
....

☀ What are my challenges?

....
....
....
....
....
....

☆ What would I like to achieve?

....
....
....
....
....
....

🌈 Positive daily affirmation: I am...

....
....
....
....
....
....

Gratitude Journal

Date: ....

❇ *Today I am grateful for:*

....

....

....

....

....

☀ *What are my challenges?*

....

....

....

....

....

☆ *What would I like to achieve?*

....

....

....

....

....

🌈 *Positive daily affirmation: I am...*

....

....

....

....

....

Gratitude Journal

Date: ....

❀ Today I am grateful for:

....
....
....
....
....
....

☀ What are my challenges?

....
....
....
....
....
....
....

☆ What would I like to achieve?

....
....
....
....
....
....

🌈 Positive daily affirmation: I am...

....
....
....
....
....
....
....

Gratitude Journal

Date: ....

✳ Today I am grateful for:

....
....
....
....
....
....

☀ What are my challenges?

....
....
....
....
....

☆ What would I like to achieve?

....
....
....
....
....

🌈 Positive daily affirmation: I am...

....
....
....
....
....
....

Gratitude Journal

Date: ....

Today I am grateful for:

What are my challenges?

What would I like to achieve?

Positive daily affirmation: I am...

Yesterday I was clever,
so I wanted to change the world.
Today I am wise
so I am changing myself.

~RUMI

Gratitude Journal

Date: ....

✽ Today I am grateful for:

....

....

....

....

....

☼ What are my challenges?

....

....

....

....

....

....

☆ What would I like to achieve?

....

....

....

....

....

🌈 Positive daily affirmation: I am...

....

....

....

....

....

Gratitude Journal

Date: ....

❋ Today I am grateful for:
....
....
....
....
....
....

☼ What are my challenges?
....
....
....
....
....
....

☆ What would I like to achieve?
....
....
....
....
....
....

◠ Positive daily affirmation: I am...
....
....
....
....
....
....

Gratitude Journal

Date: ....

❋ Today I am grateful for:

....

....

....

....

....

☀ What are my challenges?

....

....

....

....

....

☆ What would I like to achieve?

....

....

....

....

....

🌈 Positive daily affirmation: I am...

....

....

....

....

....

Gratitude Journal

Date: ....

❁ Today I am grateful for:

....
....
....
....
....

☀ What are my challenges?

....
....
....
....
....

☆ What would I like to achieve?

....
....
....
....
....

🌈 Positive daily affirmation: I am...

....
....
....
....
....

Gratitude Journal

Date: ....

❀ Today I am grateful for:

....
....
....
....
....

☀ What are my challenges?

....
....
....
....
....

☆ What would I like to achieve?

....
....
....
....
....

🌈 Positive daily affirmation: I am...

....
....
....
....
....
....

Treasure the love
you receive above all.
It will survive long after
your gold and good health
have vanished.

~OG MANDINO

Gratitude Journal

Date: ....

✿ Today I am grateful for:

....
....
....
....
....

☀ What are my challenges?

....
....
....
....
....

☆ What would I like to achieve?

....
....
....
....
....

🌈 Positive daily affirmation: I am...

....
....
....
....
....

Gratitude Journal

Date: ....

❋ Today I am grateful for:

....
....
....
....
....
....

☀ What are my challenges?

....
....
....
....
....
....

☆ What would I like to achieve?

....
....
....
....
....
....

🌈 Positive daily affirmation: I am...

....
....
....
....
....
....

Gratitude Journal

Date: ....

❋ Today I am grateful for:

....
....
....
....
....

☀ What are my challenges?

....
....
....
....
....

☆ What would I like to achieve?

....
....
....
....
....

🌈 Positive daily affirmation: I am...

....
....
....
....
....

Gratitude Journal

Date: ....

✾ Today I am grateful for:

....
....
....
....
....
....

☀ What are my challenges?

....
....
....
....
....
....

☆ What would I like to achieve?

....
....
....
....
....
....

🌈 Positive daily affirmation: I am...

....
....
....
....
....
....

Gratitude Journal

Date: ....

❋ Today I am grateful for:

....
....
....
....
....
....

☀ What are my challenges?

....
....
....
....
....
....

☆ What would I like to achieve?

....
....
....
....
....
....

〰 Positive daily affirmation: I am...

....
....
....
....
....
....

Gratitude Journal

Date: ....

❀ Today I am grateful for:

....
....
....
....
....
....

☀ What are my challenges?

....
....
....
....
....
....

☆ What would I like to achieve?

....
....
....
....
....
....

🌈 Positive daily affirmation: I am...

....
....
....
....
....
....

Gratitude Journal

Date: ....

❀ Today I am grateful for:

....
....
....
....
....
....

☼ What are my challenges?

....
....
....
....
....
....

☆ What would I like to achieve?

....
....
....
....
....

⌒ Positive daily affirmation: I am...

....
....
....
....
....
....

Gratitude Journal

Date: ....

❀ Today I am grateful for:

....
....
....
....
....

☼ What are my challenges?

....
....
....
....
....

☆ What would I like to achieve?

....
....
....
....
....

🌈 Positive daily affirmation: I am...

....
....
....
....
....

Gratitude Journal

Date: ....

✳ Today I am grateful for:

....
....
....
....
....

☀ What are my challenges?

....
....
....
....
....

☆ What would I like to achieve?

....
....
....
....
....

◠ Positive daily affirmation: I am...

....
....
....
....
....

Gratitude Journal

Date: ....

❋ Today I am grateful for:

....
....
....
....
....
....

☀ What are my challenges?

....
....
....
....
....
....

☆ What would I like to achieve?

....
....
....
....
....
....

◠ Positive daily affirmation: I am...

....
....
....
....
....
....

Gratitude Journal

Date: ....

❀ Today I am grateful for:

....

....

....

....

....

☼ What are my challenges?

....

....

....

....

....

☆ What would I like to achieve?

....

....

....

....

....

◠ Positive daily affirmation: I am...

....

....

....

....

....

Gratitude Journal

Date: ....

❀ Today I am grateful for:

....
....
....
....
....

☀ What are my challenges?

....
....
....
....
....

☆ What would I like to achieve?

....
....
....
....
....

🌈 Positive daily affirmation: I am...

....
....
....
....
....
....

Made in the USA
Middletown, DE
16 June 2021